Really David!

An Autobiography

David R Morgan

Illustrated by Anastasia Kotelnikova

Really David!

An Autobiography

This is a work of fiction.

Text and Illustrations copyrighted

by David Morgan ©2020

Library of Congress Control Number: 2020912506

All rights reserved. No part of this book may be reproduced, transmitted, or stored in an information retrieval system in any form or by any means, graphic, electronic, or mechanical without prior written permission from the author.

Printed in the United States of America

A 2 Z Press LLC

PO Box 582

Deleon Springs, FL 32130

bestlittleonlinebookstore.com

sizemore3630@aol.com

440-241-3126

ISBN: 978-1-946908-45-2

Dedication

To Bex and Toby,
Who are the
most important part of
my autobiography!

My story began in 1955,
for childhood is a cherished thing,
It plays a big role in the wonder
and adventure that life can bring.

My mum, Joanna, was a writer who helped run London University. My dad, Richard, was a nurseryman and painted pictures of pure beauty!

In 1960, we moved from London to Hertfordshire and to River Hall. That, I would declare, was the start of it all! "Really, David!" exclaimed my parents as they watched as I played my curious games. "It's Vizit's idea!" I would say. My imaginary friend was the one I always blamed.

My childhood was filled with fun - so many dogs and cats and fantasy,
For River Hall was truly a place where any child could be happy.

With mum and dad close and always lending a helping hand,
My childhood as an only child turned into a magical land.

"Really, David!" is what mum and dad would often say, when my great imagination would affect the way that I would play.

And one day Vizit jumped so very, very high,
He jumped right through a hole in the empty sky.
He waved his hand as he sat
upon a shooting star, and I watched
him ride away into the
distance so very far.

It wasn't that I was not smart, nor that I was not slick,
It is simply that I was different and a bit dyslexic.

And my first dog, Rusty, so affectionately licked my face,
  At the tender age of seven, everything fit in its place.

Rusty's hair shone so lovely golden in the bright sunlight,
And we laid lazily together after playing with all our might.

My boy Rusty came to collect me right after my day at school,
He was a friend and constant companion - a dog's one and only rule!

I cherished spending the day at the local village fair, and had such fun on rides and won my goldfish, Lucky, there.

On other fun days it was off to the cinema with mum I'd go,
For 'Jason and the Argonauts' or 'Dorothy and her rainbow.'

"Really, David!" Oh, how I loved sausage sandwiches with fried baked beans,
And mayonnaise, yes lots! - it was so much tastier than it seems.

And I was mad about melted chocolate on coconut ice cream,
Candy floss, soft toffees, and milkshakes frothed up like a dream!

Mum made Christmas marvelous and magical and she truly did believe,
And with dad's help, we decorated together till late on Christmas Eve.

At Boxing Day lunch, Uncle Frank's laughter the room would fill,
Because he would shoot chipolata sausages out of each nostril!!

On school holidays, I hung with a
Superhero, whose glasses broke,
And our friend Space Girl also
wore lenses and loved a good joke.

As I grew, I treasured time at the seaside,
where waves crashed and grabbed-
I searched rock pools for Dahlia
anemones, shells, and the odd crab,
My mum and dad believed
a child did not belong in a mold,
That, like me, each should be
allowed the time to grow and
their true self unfold.

In my later stories, through William Whipper-Snapper and Emma's eyes, I saw a cozy Victorian world, where the children discovered an enchanted 1 B Prize - The prize caused so many curious things to happen and before not very long, I wrote how that 1 B Prize granted wishes that would go hilariously wrong.

Then, my writing returned to Elizabethan times - 1066 and Norman dealings,
To Pre-Roman Britain and numerous, astounding happenings,
Silly ghosts play tricks, Green Jinntars attack, and a dancing Dream-Creator,
Then on to a mysterious planet and the Merry Prize-Maker!

I also imagined a magical music
tape whose tune could take me,
To a far away world and a land called Harmony.
But this land was at war with
the feared Discords of Din,
It was such an exciting, melodious adventure
to take part in.

As I look back at those years at my beloved River Hall,
I want to thank you, mum and dad - you gave me your all.
A happy childhood is made up of more than just one magical day,
It is a chest of good memories that no one can take away.

Now, my own children, Bex and Toby, are like wizardry,
They bring back that special magic in my life for me.
And sometimes they take my same old diamond spoon,
To eat a piece of their very own cherry pancake moon.

But listen! Those baked beans in mayonnaise are singing cantatas, and that sausage has been left in charge of those naughty chipolatas. "To be Frank, it's time David," laughed the sausage, "to grow up, really!" "Yes, sausage, I know. I am 65 and I have grown up... well, nearly!"

The End
For Now

Write Your Own Autobiography

1. What is your name?

2. How old are you?

3. Write about your parents and brothers and sisters if you have them.

4. What are your favorite things to do? Swimming? Baseball? Skating? More?

5. Tell where you live and about your home and bedroom.

6. What is your favorite subject if you are in school.

7. What is your favorite food?

8. What is your favorite book?

My About Your Own Autobiography

9. What is your favorite color or colors?

10. Do you have a favorite pet?

11. What is your favorite song?

12. Have you ever taken a vacation? Was it fun?

13. What was the best day you ever had?

14. If you could imagine doing anything in the world, what would it be?

15. What is your favorite thing to do with your friends?

16. Do you have a favorite movie?

17. What do you want to be when you grow up?

David R Morgan lives in England. He is a talented full time teacher and writer.

He has written music journalism, poetry and children's books. His books for children include : 'The Strange Case of William Whipper-Snapper', three 'Info Rider' books for Collins and 'Blooming Cats' which won the Acorn Award and was animated for television. He has also written a Horrible Histories biography : 'Spilling The Beans On Boudicca' and stories for Children's anthologies.

For the last 4 years he has been working on his Soundings Project with his son Toby, performing his own poetry/writing to Toby's original music. This work is on YouTube, Spotify and Soundcloud.

Other Books by David R. Morgan

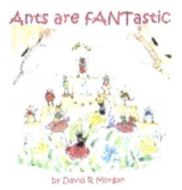 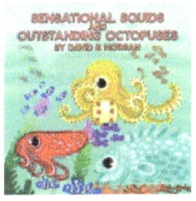   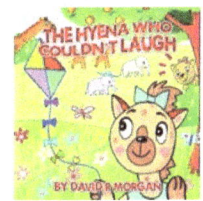
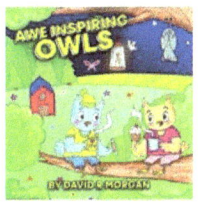  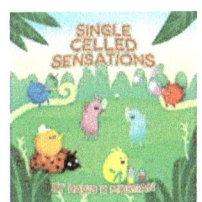 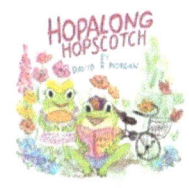 
    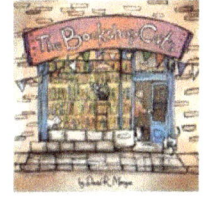
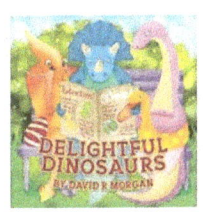    

And many more to come!

A2Z Press LLC

A2Z Press LLC published this work. A2Z Press LLC is a publishing company created by Terrie Sizemore for the purpose of publishing literary works by new and aspiring writers. All content is G-rated. We welcome your submissions of ideas for children's literature as well as adult and self-help topics. Science and medicine, holidays and other interesting topics are all welcome. Submit queries to sizemore3630@aol.com or PO Box 582 Deleon Springs, FL 32130

Visit our Website

Visit terriesizemorestoryteller.com or bestlittleonlinebookstore.com for our latest titles and gifts for everyone.

www.ingramcontent.com/pod-product-compliance
Lightning Source LLC
Chambersburg PA
CBHW051400110526
44592CB00023B/2902